21st
Century
Skills Libra

HEALTHY FOR LIFE

RUNNING

Ellen Labrecque

Cherry Lake Publishing
Ann Arbor, Michigan

Published in the United States of America by Cherry Lake Publishing
Ann Arbor, MI
www.cherrylakepublishing.com

Content Adviser: Thomas Sawyer, EdD, Professor of Recreation and Sports Management,
Indiana State University, Terre Haute, Indiana

Library of Congress Cataloging-in-Publication Data
Labrecque, Ellen.
  Running / by Ellen Labrecque.
     p. cm.
  ISBN-13: 978-1-60279-021-6 (lib.bdg.)   978-1-60279-089-6 (pbk.)
  ISBN-10: 1-60279-021-3 (lib. bdg.)   1-60279-089-2 (pbk.)
  1. Running. 2. Running—Training. I. Title.
  GV1061.L22 2008
  613.7'172—dc22   2007003894

Cherry Lake Publishing would like to acknowledge the work of
The Partnership for 21st Century Skills.
Please visit www.21stcenturyskills.org *for more information.*

TABLE OF CONTENTS

CHAPTER ONE

INTRODUCTION TO RUNNING

Running is good for your body and your mind.

Imagine yourself outside on a beautiful fall day. You are jogging on a path in the woods. The sun is shining, and the leaves on the trees are orange and gold. The wind tousles your hair, and you can hear fallen leaves crunch under your feet. The fresh air fills up your lungs. You feel free as a bird. In fact, when you pick up speed, you feel like you can soar into the air. Ahhh, running—it makes you feel happy to be alive!

Running is one of the best and simplest forms of exercise. It helps to keep your muscles strong, your heart and lungs healthy, and your body **lean**. You can run anywhere—in the woods, through a field, on the playground, on a track, or on a city sidewalk. And besides a good pair of running shoes, you don't need much other equipment to get started. Best of all, running is a sport for everybody: grade school kids, teenagers, college students, and healthy men and women. All right, it's time to lace up those shoes. Let's learn about running.

Life & Career Skills

Running is a great way to learn self-direction. Because running is a sport you can do on your own, you can learn and develop at your own pace. You set your own goals, and it's up to you to set aside the time and energy to devote to meeting those goals.

Running is a great physical sport for everyone.

CHAPTER TWO

EQUIPMENT AND SAFETY

Whether you are a beginner or an expert runner, running shoes are the most important equipment you need. Running is a simple sport, but the pounding motion puts stress on your legs and feet. Because of this, it is

For runners, having the right type of running shoes is key.

Running shoes must fit well to help prevent injury.

important to buy the right running shoes. If you are a beginning runner, it is smart to visit a running store in your area. The salesperson will help you pick a pair of running shoes that are comfortable and will help you stay injury free (see sidebar on page 29).

Once you have running shoes picked out, take a look at some other equipment that can be helpful (see sidebar on page 10 for ideas on how to use what you already have for equipment):

• Running watch with heart monitor feature: A digital wristwatch with a stopwatch function tells you how long or how fast you are running per a certain distance. A wristwatch with a heart monitor feature also tells you if your heart is beating too fast, too slow, or just right to gain the most fitness benefits from your workout. A watch with a heart monitor costs about $100.

A digital stopwatch is a great way to time how fast you can run.

Be sure to wear a hat and mittens when you run on cold days.

• Hat and mittens: If you live in a cold area, it is important to dress
warmly during the winter months. More than 70 percent of your
body heat escapes through your head and hands. If you get cold easily,
it is worth buying gear made for skiers. A ski-type hat ($30) and ski-
type mittens ($30 to $100) will give you the extra warmth you need.

Learning & Innovation Skills

Everybody wants the coolest equipment for sports, but it doesn't always make sense to spend a lot of money. Often clothing and gear you already have work just as well as new stuff. What do you have at home that can serve the same purpose? Here are some tips for running equipment alternatives.

- Socks instead of mittens: Layer your hands with a couple pairs of socks to keep your fingers warm! Wool socks are the warmest of all.

- Bright clothing instead of a reflective vest: Wearing light-colored clothing will help drivers see you. White is the best color, but bright yellow and orange colors work, too.

- Hooded sweatshirt instead of a hat: Pull the hood around your head and use the strings to tie it tight. Just make sure you can see on both sides of you.

- **Reflective** gear and headlamp: If you plan to run at night, a reflective vest will help you be more visible to passing cars. Instead of wearing a reflective vest, some runners wear reflective stripes on their arms and legs. Drivers are more likely to see the reflected light if it's moving. If you run away from traffic, where there are no streetlights, a headlamp will allow you to see through the darkness. The vest costs about $15, a reflective armband is about $3, and a headlamp costs about $40. They can all be bought at sporting goods stores.

CHAPTER THREE

TRAINING

Runners come in all shapes and sizes, and they perform on all different skill levels. They can generally be put into three different categories: beginners, amateurs, and professionals.

Not all runners are the same. They perform on many different skill levels.

You're never too young to start running.

Beginners are runners who are just starting out. They don't know a lot about the sport. Amateur runners know more than beginners. They usually run three or more times a week and time their runs. Sometimes, they enter road races on the weekends. Professional runners get paid to run. They follow strict training schedules and watch their diet closely. The pros enter races all over the world, and their goal is to win. The more races they win, the more money they make.

If you are just beginning a running program, the smartest way to start training is by walking. The editors at *Runner's World* magazine suggest a run-walk routine. Run for thirty seconds, walk until you catch your breath,

Life & Career Skills

Paula Radcliffe is one of the world's best runners, but fans admire Radcliffe as more than a leader in the sport. They also admire her for her commitment in the face of failure and disappointment. At the 2004 Olympics in Athens, Greece, she was the favorite to win the marathon and the 10,000-meter race. But, suffering from stomach pains, she dropped out of both races.

Radcliffe was devastated, but she wasn't about to give up on her goals. Just three months after the Summer Games, she came back to win the 2004 New York Marathon.

"The time didn't matter today," she said after the race. "What mattered was winning."

Radcliffe plans to win gold in the marathon at the 2008 Games. Four years after that, she also plans to win gold in the 2012 Summer Games in London, England, her home country.

Maybe she will win a gold medal, or maybe she won't. But one thing is for sure: she'll keep going for it—again and again.

run for another thirty seconds, and repeat. Try this walk-run plan for twenty to thirty minutes. As you build up your strength, try running for one minute, take a break, and repeat. Try to keep increasing the time you are running and decreasing the time you are walking. Your goal should be to eventually run thirty minutes without taking a break.

When you begin your running program, plan to work out at least three times a week. With this frequency, your muscles and lungs will get stronger. You'll soon notice yourself becoming more fit.

One of the biggest mistakes that beginner runners make is running too fast. Running too fast makes you feel breathless and causes your legs to burn. At first, try running at the pace of a fast walk.

"The talk test is a simple way to judge your pace," writes Amby Burfoot, executive editor of *Runner's World*, in his book *Complete Book*

*Running with a friend is a great way to enjoy
the sport and keep yourself motivated.*

Collaborating with
a friend can benefit
you both. Before you
get started, sit down
together and draw up
a training program you
both can stick to. Be
sure to communicate
your goals with each
other so you can
develop a program that
meets both your needs.
Because you and your
training partner will
have different strengths,
you can help each
other improve. Be
open to changes to
your program as you
both meet and exceed
your personal goals
so you can move
towards new ones.

of Running. "Aim to run at a comfortable pace that you can still talk to your training partner while running." If you are breathing too hard to talk, you need to slow down.

When you begin a running routine, train with a friend. Running with a friend will help you stay committed to your training program. If you know someone is waiting for you at the track, you're less likely to tell yourself you're too busy to run. A friend can encourage you to keep going when you want to stop. A friend can also run for help if you get hurt. Most important, training with a friend makes running more fun. The more you enjoy running, the more you will run!

Safe Places to Run

*All-purpose trails are designed to accommodate
walkers, runners, and bikers.*

Ride around town on a bike early on a Saturday morning, and you'll
be sure to pass a runner. The ease of being able to walk out your door
and start training is too good to pass up. But the pounding on concrete

21st Century Content

No matter how careful you are, you can still get injured while running. If you experience pain during or after a run, take a break from your routine until the pain is gone. Pain is a sign that something is wrong! Ice a sore muscle several times daily for a few days. Rest an aching joint. If you do not feel any improvement after a few days, make an appointment with your doctor.

sidewalks can cause aches and pains in your legs. Running on the asphalt street is softer but can be dangerous because of busy traffic. You can also jog through the woods. This journey can be relaxing and peaceful. But you have to be careful not to stumble over roots, plants, rocks, or fallen branches (see sidebar on page 18).

Running through nature trails or the woods requires you to be cautious of the natural conditions of the trail.

For beginners, running on a treadmill is the best way to start out.

If you are a beginner runner, we advise you to stick with track and treadmill workouts at first. They are the smartest and safest choices.

The best part about running on a track is the smooth and soft surface. You don't have to worry about tripping over curbs, roots, or uneven sidewalks. Most important, tracks are safe and free from speeding cars, trucks, and buses. When you run on a track, you only have to worry about one thing: running.

The treadmill is also a good place to train, especially on rainy days. Like tracks, treadmills are soft, so your legs won't take too much of a beating. Plus treadmills are precise: you'll know exactly how many miles per half hour or hour you run. Running on a treadmill does take a little while to master. At first, ask a trainer or teacher to help you, and be sure to keep the speed on low. Once you get the hang of it, then you can go a little faster.

CHAPTER FIVE

HEALTH BENEFITS

Running can be a great way to get in shape and meet new people.

You now know how to run, where to run, and what to wear while running. Now you will learn *why* running is so good for you. Amby Burfoot said, "I run for recreation, stress relief, weight control, camaraderie, health, the challenge, and many other reasons."

Running can help people increase their stamina.

He is right—running is beneficial in all these ways. First, running helps you maintain a healthy weight. You burn 500 to 900 calories per hour by running, depending on your weight and speed. You only burn 75 to 100 calories per hour playing video games.

Second, running helps keep your bones and muscles strong. Running also lowers your chances for developing cancer, heart disease, and high blood pressure. Jogging has proven to simply make people feel happier.

Clearly, running has many health benefits. But it is still important to eat properly when you're in

21st Century Content

Ever wonder about how many calories you burn when bowling? Dancing? Check out this chart to see about how many calories per hour you burn doing different activities. Keep in mind that each number is based on a person who weighs 100 pounds (45.3 kilograms). If you weigh more, you'll burn a little more; if you weigh less, you'll burn less.

ACTIVITY	Approximate Number of Calories Burned Per Hour
Running	500
Playing soccer	400
Dancing	300
Riding a bicycle	250
Skateboarding	230
Bowling	138
Playing video games	48
Writing	50
Reading	50

a running program. Nancy Clark, a sports nutritionist, offers three basic keys to healthy eating in her book, *Sports Nutrition Guidebook:*

- Make sure your diet has lots of variety. "There is no one magic food," she says.
- Eat small amounts. There is room in your diet for candy or chips. But eat small amounts of junk food, and make sure you eat fruits and vegetables as well.

Chips and candy should only be eaten in small amounts.

Sliced apples are a great healthy snack.

21st Century Content

Healthy snacks don't have to be boring! All you need to make a healthy snack is healthy ingredients. Get some friends together to brainstorm ideas on how to come up with fun new treats. Here's a list of some good ingredients to get you started:

- peanut butter
- fresh fruits
- fresh vegetables
- plain popcorn
- dried fruit
- nuts & seeds
- granola
- whole-grain crackers or bread
- yogurt
- lunch meat
- salsa
- pretzels
- whole-grain cereal
- applesauce

• Finally, choose natural over packaged food. "For instance," Clark says, "choose apples rather than apple juice and baked potatoes over potato chips."

Water is the most important ingredient in a runner's diet. It helps your body get rid of waste and helps you convert food into energy. Drinking water also helps an athlete combat dehydration, which produces symptoms of tiredness, overheating, and muscle cramps. And check this out: 70 percent of the human body is made up of water! You should try to carry a bottle of water with you when you run, and then guzzle more afterward as well. Drink up—it does a runner good!

Clark makes one more important point: a runner should drink lots of water daily. "Water is the most important **nutrient** in your sports diet," she says. On average, an inactive person who doesn't exercise should drink about eight glasses of water daily. Runners should try to drink at least nine or ten glasses a day.

Runners should drink plenty of water to stay healthy and properly hydrated.

The best way for you to stay in shape is to keep running. The best way to keep running is to stay injury free. Here are five important tips that will keep you healthy and on your feet.

1. Stay flexible: Stretching after your run is key to healthy running. Stretching increases your range of motion, improves your coordination, and promotes better circulation. Here are some stretching tips that will help you to prevent injuries.

   • When stretching, move slowly and gently. Stretching is not a race, so relax and don't forget to breathe!

   • Hold each stretch for about thirty seconds. If you have a particularly tight muscle or a problem area that you want to stretch a little longer, hold the stretch for up to sixty seconds.

   • Stretching should never be painful. If a stretch hurts, you are pushing or pulling too hard on your muscles. Ease up a bit.

21st Century Content

Buying running shoes can be overwhelming. There are so many choices! Plus running shoes can cost anywhere from $30 to $150. Whatever your budget is, you can find a suitable pair of shoes. Just follow these basic guidelines:

• Buy running shoes from a running store. The salespeople can steer you toward the best shoes for you.

• Make sure the salesperson measures both feet. Most people have one foot that is bigger than the other. Your shoes should fit the bigger foot.

• Take shoes out for a test run before you buy them. (Most stores allow you to do so.) This way, you can feel shoes in action.

• Once you found your pair, buy the same brand the next time.

Stretching after running is a necessary step to avoid injury.

2. Rest: A common mistake for beginner runners is to run every day without taking a break. The more tired your legs are, the more prone you are to twisted knees and ankles. Give yourself a day or two for your legs to chill and rejuice. They've earned it!

3. Be smart *where* you run: Stick with smooth, level, soft surfaces when training. This type of surface will ease the stress on your legs and prevent overuse injuries, such as shin splints, from slowing you down.

4. Be smart when you run: Take a break or run inside on a treadmill *when* the temperatures are extremely hot or cold. During the summer months when it is about 85 degrees and 90 percent humidity, running can be dangerous. Your body has too hard of a time cooling itself off,

and you can suffer from heat stroke. If you really want to run on these warm days, try to do it early in the morning or in the evening when the sun isn't as bright. During the winter months, if the temperature is below freezing and the wind chill is in the single digits, it's best to stay inside. You could suffer from hypothermia, which causes shivering and tiredness, and you can even pass out. If you do run on these cold days, dress in lots of layers and run in the middle of the day, when the sun is brightest and provides the most warmth.

5. Warm up before and cool down after each run. You can warm up before a run by walking slowly. *Gradually,* walk a little faster until your leg muscles feel loose enough to jog. After a run, you should also take a slow walk to cool down.

You are finally ready to hit the track. But just remember: above all else, running is fun! So what are you waiting for? Ready. Set. Go!

Before starting a running program, talk to your doctor for more advice on how to prevent injury. Common running injuries include:
- blisters
- ankle sprains
- dizziness
- achilles tendonitis
- plantar fasciitis
- shin splints
- muscle pulls
- runner's knee
- stress fractures
- Iliotibial band syndrome

GLOSSARY

camaraderie (cahm-uh-RAHD-uhr-ee) friendship between people who share an activity or experience

heat stroke (HEET STROHK) a serious medical condition caused by exposure to extreme heat

hypothermia (hye-puh-THUR-mee-uh) a serious medical condition caused by exposure to extreme cold

lean (LEEN) having little extra fat beyond what the body needs to function at its best

marathon (MARE-uh-thon) a 26.2-mile race

nutrient (new-TREE-ent) a substance that is needed for a plant or animal to stay strong and healthy

reflective (ree-FLEK-tiv) able to reflect light

routine (ROO-teen) part of a regular pattern of activity

stress (STRES) pressure or strain on an object

treadmill (TRED-mil) a machine with an endless belt where somebody can walk, jog, or run at a controlled speed and elevation

FOR MORE INFORMATION

Books

Burfoot, Amby, ed. *Complete Book of Running*. Emmaus, PA: Rodale Press, 2004.

Clark, Nancy. *Nancy Clark's Sports Nutrition Guidebook*. 3rd ed. Champaign, IL: Human Kinetics Publishers, 2003.

Galloway, Jeff. *Galloway's Book on Running*. Bolinas, CA: Shelter Publications, Inc., 2002.

Web Sites

Runner's World magazine

www.runnersworld.com

For stories about training, gear, and more

Paula Radcliffe's official Web site

www.paularadcliffe.com

A site about the world's fastest female marathoner

Cool Running

www.coolrunning.com

An online resource for runners of all abilities

KidsHealth

www.kidshealth.org

Providing health information about kids

INDEX

ABOUT THE AUTHOR

Ellen Labrecque is a freelance writer living outside of New York City. Previously, she was a senior editor for eight years at *Sports Illustrated For Kids* magazine. An avid runner, Ellen awakes at 5 A.M. to log some miles before beginning her day.